nothing to declare

For Emma, Reni, Jo, Christina and Lesley. And Dick the Vet.

nothing to declare

MAGS WEBSTER

PUNCHER & WATTMANN

First published in 2020
Published by Puncher and Wattmann
PO Box 279
Waratah NSW 2298
http://www.puncherandwattmann.com
puncherandwattmann@bigpond.com

ISBN 9781925780987

A catalogue record for this book is available from the National Library Australia.

Cover design by Ryan Stephenson
Typeset by Christine Bruderlin and Brenda Thornley
Text set in Adobe Garamond Pro
Printed by Lightning Source International

This project has been assisted by the Australian Government through the Australia Council, its arts funding and advisory body.

Contents

I

I know you'd rather I stayed hidden

Hybrid

once I was half flower, half self
                Alice Oswald

I am half flower, half self; I grow a spathe
to wrap you in a perfumed hood; my roots
spread in your skin; my cells pulse xylem
through your veins. You seek me like a bee;
you bumble the ferment of my smell, butt
at the pollen-stippled core, where spheres
encrusted with soft stings wait to latch
onto your limbs. I hold you, ripened, trap
your cries like lacewings in my hair. Into
my mouth falls night-fruit, torn apart; it tastes
of you, such tender inflorescence. Now *you*
are the flower, and I the bee find I cannot
lift my head; I lap the nectar at your gist
and drown as your petals close.

Bonnard beauty reveals all

Hey ho, it's bath time—again.
    I must be
the cleanest muse
    in Christendom, not
a fleck of paint

    on my flesh, unless
a slash of cadmium
    on his canvas. He has
this kink: that I must
    undress and cover myself

in water. I recline against
    its lapping tongues, my legs
so decorously crossed, until
    the steam has quite
died down. Then he whispers *time*—

    it's time to cover yourself
up. But the ochre's wet
    on the tip of his brush,
and my body takes time to dry.
    He'll work on me

until late at night, long after
    the bath has cooled. He'll
expunge my puckered skin,
    my flaking nails, as he dabs
at my breasts

and thighs. I recede into
a wash of stipple and blur,
    as if he's swabbing all
the woman from the frame.
    When I take the towel

from his outstretched hand,
    it's the only time his eyes
can meet mine.

The Blue Hour

Half-moon,
stopped dead

above the trees,
hour before

the child's cry.
In pre-dawn

trance, she goes
straight to the desk,

sandblast of words,
first ink: stinging nib

out loud from
the wound,

bloodjetting
brings relief—

night's sour humours
foam from her skin

till daylight brings
its sharpening

and the tall dark shape
of the yew tree

turns back into a yew

Dolores

Some say all it takes
is a butterfly's wing
nudging tropical skies,

and over the Arctic's
ice-rimmed scalp, winds
build torque, distended
clouds start coiling.

A motion so slight
can uncouple the world
like the sibilance

of fingers in the leaves
of a book, the stroke
of grass on a young girl's
thigh, as she lifts her hem

to show you all of the prairie,
distant sierras, the universe
shrunk to a compound eye

so when you both cry out,
you pierce the stillness
of air, and its flinch
plays back the name of pain.

Metabolising Heathcliff

after Liz Lochhead

She hoards him, cures
him in the scullery
of her soul, she feels

him flesh her,
rise like dough
beneath her skin—

she feasts from him,
he is her food,
her gruel, she will refuse

all other sustenance.
A reckling of the moors,
she understands

the way the rain is glue,
how silvery enzymes
cling the membrane

of the sky, her brain
is leavened
by rock and bog

her breath, his breath
is proved
from knotted tors

a prototype of pain,
he is the yeast
she bonds with bone

he locks
into the helmet
of her hips,

she walks
the Heights
she's yet to name

his home. She
churns the page
with iron gall,

disgorges him,
the forcemeat of
her craving, her denial.

Inside the ghost mind

One need not be a Chamber—to be Haunted—
                              Emily Dickinson

I've seen her, bent
at work, her skull
        a carnival of bees,

how she glows
in her pale moth body.
        Her desk,

a square of lamplight,
faces west. At dusk,
        she hems

the edge of day, pleats
each seed of syllable
        deep—she keeps

her tinder wit
from cooling into shadow.
        The curtains drawn,

she starts to lace
her thoughts
        into corsets

and then gowns. Her
nib's a needle,
        stitching lines

so they leak
no surplus words.
 Night inspires

her lexicons, Darkness
is her muse. Truth
 is salt, it seams

her words with terse
preservative. Inside
 each phrase

she seals herself,
behind herself concealed.
 She treads the rafters

of my brain—the blue
buzz of my mind.
 She pauses behind

my retinas, I feel her cool
regard. Then her fingertips
 brush past my brow,

and she slants her small
curved smile. *I'm Nobody* she
 whispers—*Who are You?*

Digging up Persephone

When I pulled you from Earth
you were sticky with worm casts,
your torso a brindle of glistening trails,
a map glazed by mourning. You tried
to cover yourself with your hand,
with your hair, but Death had made
you beautiful—you did not need to hide.
You lifted your head, and you smiled at me,
your mouth placental with pomegranate seeds,
a spatter of shrapnel torn from the fruit,
and I kissed your brow, as I always do
at this time of year. Once, you would clamber
up through the clay, but this time I had to
exhume you. Your surrogate, Earth,
would not give you up, she wanted your body
to fold into hers, and though jealous,
I understand why. Up here the seasons
are fevered and harsh, the air holds close
its embargo of rain. This world is no place
for a daughter of mine. Yet each dearth
you conquer, your white arms outstretched.
You have no need of a mother, a mid-wife.
You force yourself up from the womb
of the grave: a lady who rises, red hair ablaze.

A season of dryness

She who held the seasons in her gift
now finds, year round, her mood is autumn,
mauve and leaf mould, accent of frost.

Hoarding the summer heat inside, she
stares down the sun as it dies each day, she is
the final mourner keening at the grave.

Slowly withering from within, she will not speak,
but cultivates economy like seeds, lest she lose
more moisture through the harvest of words.

This silence grows her, gravid with anger, she thinks
of her daughter, wintering beneath her feet, living
a rhizome life. Pale hands reach up, dowsing

for the roots of a vernal rain, but this is still a season
of dryness, its deckled edge resists the quickening
of spring. She has promised her daughter:

Death will not work you loose from me
but each year burns off more of her power,
makes it harder to ripen the fields. Summer was all

she longed for once, but now she fears this stranger,
salt-edged and poisoned, nursing a derelict womb,
her golden-eared children pounded to dust.

Jessie from the Golden Shovel

after Gwendolyn Brooks

It's dawn. Dirty light brings us into focus, the pit where we
shared blood and skin dissolves into a bed again, sheds its surreal
armour. Your shoulders pinch into the pillows, sheets that are cool

at last, again. Almost erased by sleep, I look at you in awe.
The fading tan, the trace of last month's scars, the soft cleft
at the base of your spine. The mouth which gave commands,
　　was school-

ma'am stern, then wavered as the night grew cruel. What were we
in that dark? We're not those beings now, the morning's washed
　　the lurk
and shadow from the room, but I can still see bruises—they dilate

like hungry flowers. This is the time of day I like, before we
humans grow a carapace; we're still naked and unshelled, yet to strike
out of our night-selves. It's when I'm likely to be truthful, and straight-

away, you wake. Your eyes film me, they track and bring me close-up.
　　We
are unrehearsed, we don't know what to do, so we start kissing, kissing
like we're being paid—or I'm the mark and you're the irresistible
　　assassin.

How damned natural it feels. And yet I hardly know you—first
    time we
hooked up, you left without telling me your name. Tall, blonde,
    too thin,
you were my abyss. Did you know how much I'd crave you? How
    I'd begin

to haunt the Shovel, spinning out the gins as long as I dared? *And how
    are we*
again? the barman Milt would ask, as again I described you, down to
    the jazz
tattoo on the back of your shin. *That sounds like Jessie, 'cept she OD'd
    last June.*

Who are you, woman in my bed? One thing's for sure, you'll
    never owe
me anything. Not even your name. So what if you're really dead? We
    all die
sometime, the cliché goes, and I'm on my way—I'll be there soon.
    Real soon.

Mrs Batman M.D, Msc, Psych.D

after Carol Ann Duffy

I know you'd rather I stayed
hidden, but it's time we worked
on your secrecy obsession,
how you love to go out
at night; that mask of yours—
    you must know, deep down,
    you're not fooling anyone.

You've never been much
of a talker but lately it's worse—
we should get your bio-sonar
checked—I will not be ignored.
Remember, I learned vespertilian
specially for you—so there's no
excuse. Don't give me that
    I didn't hear you—biggest
    load of guano I ever heard.

I've broken a code, I know,
must live with the consequence
of leaving the analyst's chair
to join you on the couch
(the only time you've ever stayed
horizontal) but you are such
a fascinating specimen.
    First time I saw you,
    I swear—KAPOW!!!

And besides, I'm drawn to this
nocturnal life, I love the suit
you wear, its anatomical
correctness. When you come home
after work, I like to peel you
from the rubber, put my mouth
to your liquorice skin:
>   I'm addicted to your taste,
>   the civet of darkness . . .

. . . but it's not all been moonlight
and chiropterophily. My rodent allergy
is a pain, but what can I do? They give me
heart-burn. So annoying too, about
the Batmobile. I only popped out
for cigarettes, didn't think it would
get clamped. Apologies for taking it
without asking—but could I please get
down now? I know we agreed
bats should invert the world, but
>   I can't get used to the feeling
>   of blood rushing to my head.

Anyway, all this 'upside-down'
is nothing but displacement. We
should talk about the real problem:
your speluncaphobia. How can a bat
be scared of caves? I blame it on
your mother. Did you see something
you shouldn't have when you were

young? Is that why you are
so attracted to that anorexic Cat?
     Her body couldn't hide a cave
     to save her scrawny life.

     No, not 'the square-jawed
look' again. Classic symptom
of denial. Has that Robin been
teasing you? I'll give him holy
complications. My darling little
     horseshoe, my precious
     pipistrelle, we must fix this

     for the sake of our marriage.
Night after night, you're avoiding me.
Is it because I earn more money?
Have letters after my name? All
that education—still I didn't see
this coming. Just my luck
     to fall in love with a man
who's a bat—without balls.

II

Nothing to declare

My first kiss

Was it Bill? Faded jeans, an experienced tongue—
or Tim—too tall, too shy—(but *nice*).
Or Jo? Same height, same age, same sex—
or Grace—fresh toothpaste, slow, polite.
Or was it John, the vicar's son—alleluia!—
(on my knees), or Chip, with stubble
on a rockstar chin? Was it deep and 'French'—
did my jaw go numb? Or was it furtive, rushed—
and somehow *wrong*? I remember the sound
of a saxophone, I remember the feeling
of flesh leaving bone. When I opened
up my eyes, too much light rushed in, so
I opened up my self, made the hurting begin.

First language

Night holds us
    in parenthesis

a mouth
    to mouthing

umlauts waiting
    for release

we interpret each other
    pores, scars, puckering

in pinch and lick,
    a patois fractured

slippage of
    tongue, apostrophe

of muscle
    and gut, a half-held

breath (a vowel, a chuff
    of consonant)

we sing our fetish
    of homophony until

you thrum,
    the rhythm
        unverbing me

hot milk

brim-risen   swollen
cusp of a   small boiled moon

proud flesh   lifting
to lace   to lips

a glossy caul   such scalding
to swallow   this

hot   white   tastes
salt   *sweet*   salt

such plush-
    rimmed skin

mouths are not made
to keep

things   out
only   hold things   in

Double action

You handle my body like a
gun, your thumb careful
on the trigger of my flesh. *Don't*

move, you say, *or else*—I stay
where I am, hand pressing
'pause' above your thigh. Outside,

air darkens. A tree branch rasps
the windowpane. Inside,
the clock glows greenly, ghosts

a light along the floor. *Go!* I say, *go!*
You tighten your grip. This time, who'll
be the bullet, who the wound?

you voyage my body

after Octavio Paz

surf cirrostratus
past hidden eclipses

blood-din of moon
electric disturbance

swim east in search
of a mythical sun

a petalled corona
preparing for solstice

no star cluster
to show you the way

only my body
its currents and craving

you carry your fire
right into the flood

drown in the dark
ocean world of me

your comet tail
writhing with light

Siren

a calypso   unstitched
she drifts

the minim
    of his
        dwindling eye

his king-size raft
    capsized

he wakes up-
    holstered in ham-
        mock of skin

a body systolic
    she surfs

the clean break of him
    casts a fret
        of twisted strings

an orchestral siege—
    she is scored

    from within
blood bells in her flesh

she pitches him
    deeper, sings

the restless swell
    the chafe
of dreams, the rip

    of a jagg-
ed hymn—

cinq à sept

Come to me now and loosen me
from blunt agony

                              Sappho

two hours' devotion at our shrine
        I'm drunk
                on perfume of anise
and your lustrations

sundown's lit the fuse
        between the rooftops and the sky

in this hotel room its flame
        is on my thigh
                you trace the line of glow

your tongue a blade
        of soft against the grain of skin

more golden than gold   you say . . .

then reach for your watch   your pearls
        dress in the life
                outside of me

(beautiful in your garments)

you drain the last of your Pastis
        and smile   same time
                tomorrow?

oh please
    don't leave me in the embers
of this bed

I am afraid—last night, I was set
alight and screaming
    to be freed—

only a dream
    you soothe   but you
    stacked the faggots at my feet

on your deathless face a smile
    my terrible Aphrodite

today you kissed the scars
    you made   lit fire again
beneath my skin

    I bear this pain
        I know how it will end

these afternoons *(more golden than gold)*

will dim   become
    the hours of ash
burnt offering

Late harvest wine

This is the edge of a brown beginning,
slow corrosion of colour, light turns amber and the planet dangles
                        from the hinge of the year.

I'm wandering barefoot among the vines,
last summer's Riesling held to my lips, an edge of lime and gunflint
                        on my tongue. It's not quite

midnight, skies are varicose with stars, and
old Orion's buckled up tight and reaching for his sword. Those
                        wily sisters still run free, but

I've ceased running since my blood stopped
hungering for the chase. The vineyard's heavy with autumn fruit,
                        the grapes bulge pale and foetal.

Long ago I laboured here, under a Cancer moon,
planting hope in rows I trellised to the seasons. From tiny tendrils
                        straining for the sun came the vines

which bore the most. I learned to pick the grapes
at night, how its cool preserves their 'harmony'. Last year's yield
    was low,
                        yet worth the work just to drink

the green young wine. Now when I walk this
dendrite maze, past wizened arms spread wide, there's a warping in
                        their attitude. I suspect the crops

may fail. Late harvest wines—
they may be sweet—yet in the past I've feared them. Couldn't bear
the unpicked grapes to fester

past their time. But now the noble rot's
set in, my fruit will husk and shrivel. Mould will ash the
wrinkled skins,
drain moisture from their flesh. Yet

I'll still make a rich *terroir*, though I've seen
many moons shake loose. Now let each grape gestate the taste it
was always
meant to make. This vintage is my last,

let's raise a glass of 'too late' harvest wine.

Autopsy

I do not trust the fruit
    she brought—   that woman
with surgeon's hands
    and keen forensic eye.

Such a blush of health
    you'd think
        that peach was warm

but it's not.
    The fruit bowl
surges—still life holds
    a delicate scent of death—

a *vanitas* where she'll dig
    her thumbs among
the rind and pith.

Gather round my bedside,
    watch her make a cut—
        see what
she finds inside

    that kiwi's
mohair coat—
    how the black-seed
        fringe wells up, like
stitches round a lesion?

This passion fruit—
its leathers conceal
        a curd of cells
        dividing.

Here's some bloody
        matter in the lining
of this flesh—
            the pomegranate's

detonation—note
        how the arils clot?
Get the nurse— it's the skins

I cannot bear— their serum
weeps—stains my sheets—leaves
        an ambiguous smear.

        These specimens deserved
                intensive care,

        not a scalpel
                in the morgue
                of my lap

cause of death   unclear

Nothing to declare

I thought I'd given up France
    for good, scoured the *Gauloises*
from my tongue, but still I'm avid
    for absinthe.

I am an addict
    who does not fight disease
so much as battle with the cure.
    My name is ———. I fall

in love with countries, use men
    as their proxies, at night
I spread their bodies out tight,
    let rivers unravel,

plateaus cramp, canyons open up
    like wounds. I may be exploring
different skins, but underneath,
    their geographies are just

the same, the compass needle
    lurches northwards every time.
At first, I travelled in my sleep—
    borders aren't patrolled

in dreams—I flowed from Italy
    to Mexico, carrying my cravings
like contraband. I dived down
    under, prised apart

the hemispheres with my nomadic
        need. But it wasn't enough—
waking alone on the blade
        of a cold equator—

so I've shrunk the world
        to a scarab track
where I roll my lust
        like a ball of dung

from dateline to horizon,
        change visas
with the swivel of an eye,
        invade these realms

a month or two, then deport myself,
        no forwarding address—
not even a scrap of nametag
        stuck to the teeth of the carousel

III

Pauses in transit

At four in the morning

Mid-summer, scoured light. Sun
sips from lip of hill; Venus pins

the blush of sky. Your body, tense
with dreams, lies by my side.

Until you wake, the winter
dare not come, your hands

will still be warm, you will beg
me brush your hair once more.

Pauses in transit

after Octavio Paz

Across Hong Kong
elevators rise like bubbles
to the rim of a glass. Descent

is condensation. The sky,
a tension plugged
with cloud, sweats

surface into rivulets
of steel, slicks
the wickerwork

of scaffolding.
On a concrete
cliff, a butterfly

alights, spreads
a tiny book
of papery wings,

makes a poem
on an opaque wall
thirty-nine storeys high.

Different skin

i

at the rim
of a city, poached in smog,
rice paper screen of sky

coastlines are bespoke,
land rephrased,
post scriptum

the tides sculpt runes
of abandoned shoes,
rope ampersands
and plastic cups

spider-jointed
trawlers drag
the bays, scrape
absence from
their depths

ii

here, where the cloud
emulsifies the sun

my lungs hoist
slackened flags,

make languid fans
for my heart's
dull coal, its shiver
of ash in rib-grate

iii

I wear a different
skin, a humid lucence
sweats from pores

I'm steamed *har gau,*
an oyster tipped
from the slipper
of its shell,

glazed with the moist
veneer of heat
I understand what
mouthfeel means

as the famished air
digests me

iv

in the shadow
of Lo Fu Tau
I try to open
the hand of thought

to winnow
the good grain
from the salt

I am the tree
where birds don't rest,
my roots unsure
how to grip this soil

v

two kites coast white
space overhead, make
xíngshū with their wings

I have built a hide
of lotus leaf, wrapped
myself in hay

I must learn to erase
old scripts, sift new
words from the shoreline

self-portrait

who is this pale wide
alien, edged

in stainless steel—
ladle face in-verse

scooped-up
shrimp in broth?

not a drop
of its features spilled—

a gurn from lip
to curve

so tempting—
(lift to mouth)

how good does
reflection taste?

Eating together, eating alone

after Li-Young Lee

i

Whose turn to say grace,
Mother asks. Nobody meets
her eye. Our silence is saying
we don't believe in God

as much as we believe
in food. But we've learned
how much grace it takes
to outwit a troubling hunger.
So we mouth the recipes
for 'thanks', pile our plates

with hot, fresh deceit.
Steam rises, instead of prayer.

ii

This is the way
I do it best:
    alone
      in secret
      undisturbed.

The fridge
my altar
    the toilet
      my confessional.

Several times a day
    I kneel
    before them.

Sometimes
    like a pilgrim
    praying for forgiveness.

Sometimes
    like a needle
    preying on a vein.

Scan

My body is
    an amalgam of language

on the page
    of the hospital bed.

Only doctors understand
    nulliparous . . . . . . *fibroadenoma* . . . . . .

A stethoscope edits
    my flesh, a speculum

parts and parses me.
    My muscles perform inelegant

declensions, while doctors probe
    my etymology.

Trapped between
    the signifier and signified

I am an alphabet of body parts:
    my mouth a word-starved *O*

my breasts an asymmetric
    double *U*

my thighs a beaten *V*
    that flaps out sighs

my ears a pair of *C*s
  which hear

a white-coat say
  suspicious . . . . . . *biopsy* . . . . . .

Should I lie back—just let
  those scientific tongues

get down to work on me?
  Or think instead

of Sanskrit cursive
  gently suturing skin

the palliative glide
  of Nordic rust-and-honey

up my spine, or maybe rain-
  on-soft-tin Putonghua,

 flicking sweat
  beads from my lip?

Or better still—excavate—
  from bone, from bog, from grytt

dig out some Anglo-Saxon terms
  reclaim   *my* lump   *my* cunt   *my* tit

Sinister

after Tracy Ryan

        they say the left one's
     closer to the heart
why the ring is worn
    this side

but this bastard hand—
       my unfamiliar—
     unschooled in sans serif
      is surely just an also-ran

        attendant lord
    in my body's hierarchy
not used to carrying
pens & yet—

trustee of the shadow
    self—it knows far more,
has lain attentive—
     blocking gaps the other leaves

    I sense some plot
      from this warped
         & laboured hand

     as if writing's not
       the only task
         it can be shaped for—

              how, given time,
              it will usurp
            its dextrous, favoured
                twin.

This hand

This hand lies. A fan
of bones, glove of
skin, this hand lies

in front of me, disguised
as four fingers, a palm
and one thumb. Mimic

of muscle and joint,
it grips the kettle,
crumbles the loaf,

doesn't pause
where the bread-knife
once hung

behaves as if
I don't know
what it's done.

Game

You hand it over, slippery thighs,
long, pallid body; the handspan

of ribs, no head—it looks like
the corpse of a pet. For it to fit

in the pot, we have to break its spine.
The knife is blunt so I finish

the job with my hands, feel vertebrae
snap—and feel nothing. Why do I

cook up this stew—cartilage, brain—
boiling these old bones so long?

Unforgettable smell. Meat
falling weakly from fork. You.

Fish head

I love a woman who knows how to wield a knife—
one flick and I'm sheared in half. She drowns

my body in a froth of stock, wraps my head
in cloth and hides it under her skirt. All day

she bends and stirs, makes soup for others to eat.
Soon, if she does not stop, she will start to smell

of fish. Old woman, take me home—you've earned
me. Tease each scale from my rainbowed skin, and rub

my flesh with herbs. Tonight, when they feast
on the meal we made, I will give you the very best.

Eat my eyes, my gills, my jaw, my skull
but save my cheeks for last.

IV

Recovered memory

Stasis at Oxford 130

Today is a good day to die in a freak garden accident: fall back
onto the spikes of a giant aloe, say, & expire in its healing
embrace. I'm 12,000 miles adrift from what I used to call home,
mainlining a long macchiato. A street-kerb café: an old woman
sits two seats to my left, her bun in an eight-legged spring clasp. Blue
plastic tarantula, clamped to the back of her head—or that thing in *Alien*,
sucking off John Hurt's face. A blonde in a yellow bikini smiles up at me.
When in doubt, offers her perma-tanned thigh, *make lists*. Enquires
her left breast: *Are you ever truly satisfied? Five new ways to achieve
orgasm*. Are these connected? Sure, breast & leg, but lists & lust?
I'm in doubt. Make a list. Recent addictions: weather reports,
Marmite, coffee, misery. You see, today my marriage broke up—
or was it yesterday, last month, a few years back—the moment after
I said 'I do'? I open up Cosmo bikini girl: read an article on how
to de-tox. So easy: starve until you hallucinate, then drink a
    week's-worth
of pond-weed. Maybe it'll de-tox your body, but that's not enough,
I need it to nuke my mind. Ten years. No wonder my brain's peeling
out of my skull—it's a lot to purge in one go. But this city's
made me learn how to drink really slow, I've majored in reverse
caffeine velocity. Too much & the pavement comes up to hit me.
Too little & the pavement dribbles away. So I'll have another, long
& strong, no sugar, definitely no spouse to go. Top breakup bands:
Keane   Cowboy Junkies   Everything But The Girl   Coldplay

Noon. This city is a corpse, ants running along its length. Today
tastes of grey, not yellow like Mondays used to. The tinge
of my world before love got to it. I remember when we coloured in
the days of the week, *rainbow, rainbow, rainbow*. So, I'm trying
to find the yellow again, I'm just taking apart my brain,

to see if it can be fixed. Brains look like cauliflower—
would they taste like one? I tilt my head, hear the patter
of tiny synapses. No wild brine to smell. Actually, not so much
like a cauliflower—more like jellyfish. *Rhopilema hispidum,*
a giant grey light bulb washed up on the beach. Somewhere I read
jellyfish don't have brains, instead their whole skin is a 'nerve net'.
That's how my skin feels today, an electric web, I can light
    whole worlds,
I can hear through walls. Across by the ATM, I tune in to the queue.
One man is telling another that his dog just died. *Ah well, if you're*
    gonna go . . .
that's the way to go. Just four hours where he was a bit . . . unusual.
That woman sitting opposite, she's thinking *I cannot find*
a way to mend the breeze. She looks at me like she's watching
a documentary, and I'm some country she's never been to. I know
how she feels. Last night, my taxi driver's name was Jack.
Chatty Jack. He smelt like the ex before last—same strange twist
of scent, the melody's been left out, only the bass notes boom.
Jack's in love, ten weeks so far. She lives in Hong Kong, has a daughter,
no visa, he's giving her $6000 a month, hopes she'll come over
for good. She wants babies, but at 32 he reckons *he is getting too old.*
His mother is 'appalled', he's not sure, thinks it's for real, but I can tell
he's faking it for every fare. He's got nothing, Jack. Like, I'm an expert
in love—a used car with one careless lady owner—Fiat, Subaru,
Chrysler Jeep, Holden Commodore. Loss is a cockroach that barrels
to the back of the throat, & sticks there. We start off as
    plump balloons,
end up as rags of rubber, lying on the floor. 3.15pm. This city.
How it thickens, its arteries clotted by cars. Today I woke
as if I hadn't killed my laptop the night before, & then the memory

came rushing in, filled me with cold green ocean. Sleep makes me feel
like yesterday's life is part of my violent dream. Waiter! There's a face
in my coffee. I don't want this one, bring me another. Grief gives you
a glassy look—a veneer which stops germs getting in & poison
escaping. You see yourself in a photograph, wonder when
you got trapped in its frame. It's like looking through the wrong end
of your mind, seeing Earth's dark side instead of the sun.
Recent discovery in space: a planet with four suns.
Dr Chris Lintott, University of Oxford, tells BBC News
—*it's absolutely not what we would have expected*—
but that's where he's wrong, the unexpected happens all the time,
always has. Planets sprout suns. Orgasms are *achieved*. My head
is a caulifish, growing jellyflowers. Time for some brain DIY.
I'll borrow some knives, sharpen up for surgery. Look at that—
daytime moon. One crazy bird, knows she can't hang around
any more, she must fly behind clouds, without a map, with nothing
to lose but rainseeds, & I'll be left behind in the hollering dark,
mopping up my *rhopilema*, making it into trifle, which will get up
& dance with me, do the cortical waltz. One two three, one two
three, three—to—none. List of favourite proverbs:
can think of only one, don't even know how to say it.
Mōzhe shítou guòhé. Crossing the river by feeling the stones.
But the river's getting deeper, stones are crumbling.

I'm rushing headlong to nowhere. I want to be an ant,
they live in nomadland, don't care how many suns it has.
Three—two—one? 5.35pm. All those ants on the freeway,
they're heading home. Someone tell them: wherever they left it
this morning, it won't be there anymore.

The Before & in the After

Dying wasps crawl into shoes, settle and curl
                                              Lavinia Greenlaw

The year before you leave, dying wasps
crawl into shoes, settle & curl, the garden
puts on armour, becomes a fossil of itself,
birds sing through night, the throttle
of the magpie marbling the darkness,
& I lie face to face with the waning,
a circle of bones in a scraped edge of skin.

The year after you leave, the fret begins,
summer becomes swelter, winter too wet,
while autumn and spring, angled in between
act crazily & spin about each solstice.
I do not care. You are gone where I
cannot reach, but even in the friction
of my dreams, I still hear the shape
of your voice before your body collapsed,
before its swallow dive. Your lunate voice,

like the corpse of a wasp, curved in
on itself, like one I've just found
in the heel of my shoe, & I'm shaking
the shoe by the edge of its tongue, in case
it can tell me how to release you,
take back those moments, After &
Before, moments which settle &
curl, which won't stop stinging.

Plot

Once, he needed
the soil, felt it
    thicken through
his palms,
darken in lines
    as if learned by heart—

furrow by furrow,
    the struggle of root.

Year on year
all he gleaned
was seasonal aporia.

In the absence
of any narrative,
he tried to predict
    the twist, his head

cocked skywards,
lips moving as if
    memorising clouds—

now his back
has cramped
from double-digging,
    the shunt and heave

of clods on spade,
rhyming the flare

of breath to kick
of fork.

He's done with planting
seeds, turning
soil like pages

coaxing the green
from sullen tilth,
    shoots emerging
like bookmarks—

he's back
        to the shift
and stack of logs,

pretends they
are packed down
    tight with story—

only this time,
he's in charge
    of the plot.

Movement's a poultice

Earth's a numbing to hide in. Each night
    by the side
of the road, you let silence

transfuse you, knuckle your body
    down small.
A moth in the leaves of the dark, you merge

into dirt, pray satellites can't see you. Ants
    don't care where
 asphalt ends and you begin. You wait for sunrise

to scrape you wide open, make you start moving again.
    Flat, this road,
(no matter how steep), keeps country unravelling

its lost balls of string. Travelling the tangle
    of city and town,
you work at the knots. *Why they need loosening?*

(So many voices). All your past selves, walking inside of you,
    talking outside—
none you want as a proxy. Here's one who won't

wait, marches ahead, hustles a smoke,
    replays your life,
its dead-ends and detours. But movement's

a poultice. Been walking so long, your skin's
    split wide open:
body's forgotten the feeling of hurting.

Sleeper

*Death is never far away from them. No wonder the Greeks called moths by the
same name as the soul:* psyche.   Roger Deakin

At first you are larval
hatched
into a bunching

of muscle a slow
shunt segment
by segment
closer to sleep

you must
prepare yourself
for transformation

shed the first
of many skins

inch from
what you have
outgrown

each new
nakedness
peels deeper

till in a fallow
crackled bed
scraped
from detritus of day

you lie coffined
sessile

in night-camouflage
you mimic
death

I am glad
you are restrained

though how do I know
you are not already
somewhere
taking flight

they say
wings nearest the darkness
beat faster

I know you as
a trickster

dingy footman
the uncertain
anomalous
the alchymist

and when
cocooned
you long

to escape
the pinch
of safety

your wings itch
for freedom

so when morning
comes you blunder

towards sunlight
towards the burning

Recovered memory

Spur of slipped
serif
    a jolt of brittle
        outside, in a rasp,

a kenning of a not-
    given-shape, a noise
like grass and trees
    unmouthed, long water

ripening,
    wind-flutes of   bamboo,
some kind of this-ness
    lost, a seed of many

silences begets
    its pitch
and shift, coughs a glottal

choke of stress
    the affricates align
    the soft of lauds begins
 to pattern in my mind

and I become scales
    which lip
    my skin to pearl
    and now I know

that I was there—
    zoetic in the plangent
    dark, a breathing
    through a hyoid bone

an unhatched word,
    a stuttering in
    the throat of mud,

        just as fish dried into legs
        and Earth was tamed
        by naming

V

Breathing lessons

Source

after, becoming
    this rivered shape

    silver scoliosis
snaking fields

twisting my knots
    through infant wheat

    I did not miss
my heart

or hunger, did not
    miss its ache

    no loosening hands
nor stiffening bones

did not belong
    to grief, instead

    I curved, rehearsed
new lines against

the notch
    and prompt of bank

    gave birth
to evergreen

nursed peppered threads
　　of reeds, I rocked

　　the dark wild
of the watercress.

No need for food, I
　　was summer's

　　sustenance, I fed
the clover and the oak

the season sang
　　itself through me

　　I caught the autumn's
leaves, and dampened

down their flames.
　　A cold breeze sculled

　　my skin, I slowed—
then I decembered

underground,
　　the weather's lurch

　　and shuffle crazed
my rippled head, now

I lie stagnant
    in the ice, don't want

    the thaw to pick
my locks, but leave me

silent in the earth,
    encrypted in its dirt.

    I hate the spring
when bulbs heave

from their fists of silk,
    the skies shake loose

    their ecstasies of larks
and I become unfluent

again, fouled up
    with tears. Filtering

    through the quickened
soil, I drain into another

year, reshape myself
    without the source of you.

Nostos

All through the flight you've had Cavafy
playing in your mind. Is it true that arriving here
is what you're destined for? Call it homing
rather than homecoming, for once the airport
doors seal the vacuum of miles and time,
it's as though you've never been gone.

An easterly blows from the night-washed hills,
the air is warm and soft as ironed cloth. You breathe
blue flames of eucalypt, till your body unlocks
its prodigal shape, and distance is cleansed
from your bones. Since you went away, your life
has lacked its tinder. You've tried to belong

elsewhere, gathered knowledge from scholars, bought
fine things. Laistrygonians and Cyclops,
angry Poseidon—you've carried them all
in your soul. But this place has burned in you
since birth, coloured your sleep with cochineal,
shrilled it cobalt blue, and your body tries

to pull you back, searching for the heart
it buried in the dirt, a lodestone fired
in desert and sky, cooled in the Indian Ocean.
Blue flames breathe in you. Way beyond the rim
of the airport lights, you know there's emptiness
as full as you've ever seen, where you become part

of the scansion of land, its accents of spinifex
and schist. Gorges brim with a brazen edge.

A daytime moon spreads a scallop
of lace. Hills float a ghost-hazed wave.
You wait as the bleach of afternoon
darkens to the palette of dusk. Lilac. Plum.

Russet. Silver-sage. This land
has archived colour and time, when
you press your palm against its skin,
you touch the whole earth's story.
Answering from the warmth of rock
are words which make sense of home.

Displacement

Ask yourself: would you die if writing were denied you?
                                        Rainer Maria Rilke

Such a question—as if all this
were cellular necessity
or pathological need.

Have spent today
embracing a more
benevolent disease,

attacking the roots
which, far too long,
have choked new

growth in the garden,
fancying I hear
little shrieks

as I unsheathe them
from the socket
of the ground,

piles of strange
amputations, bunches
of knuckles

a nick here and there
in cindery flesh,
such small mouths—

white as bone.
Drastic hands, what
have they been doing

down there?
Rummaging
through the soil,

manic for sap,
squeezing nutrients
from adolescent bulbs

of daffodils, say
or the crocus in
its sleeping corm

anything that still hides
the secret of itself,
is yet to blurt into flower.

Only butterflies

response to Mahmoud Darwish's 'To a Young Poet'

I have already forgotten
how to begin.
Once, books I read

wept their lines
out loud, bled ink
from broken spines,

my hands so full
of tears I could not
hold together the writing.

Now nothing is as white
as air, stained by absence
of words.

I am not the first—my mother
and my father gave me
breath, built me
into flesh

from them I learned
how I should grow,
how language should be used,

they showed me
how to tongue my way
through life, until
this silence came.

Mahmoud, you say *truth
is black*, but truth

is whatever colour
it wants. A rose,
unpetalled by a storm,

a shred of redness
in the falcon's claw.

I hoped for roads
and secrets; but all
is grit and dust
and empty shoes.

So many graves,
hills and plains,
rivers and valleys
flowering with the dead

unspeaking mouths
of poems, such
echoes of ache and lack.

Is this all of myself?
The net unpicked
of sense, the poem incomplete

where are the butterflies
you said could
make me whole?

Words are my abyss.
However loud I dream
I cannot hear,

my voice breaks
at the shape of clouds,
the excess of the stars,

it flares, won't learn
what stillness
means, how distance
brings things nearer.

But then you talk of
love, and lilies start
to speak in syllables
of wings. Rapture

upon rapture rising,
perfect in
completeness.

Reclaiming

Once, this scarp was brim,
    edge   of fathoms, neither
land nor water, elision
    of drift and overlap

    of solid, stealing water,
erasure, rephrasing
    eloquence of inundation
        sound making sense
of depth,   limning
    the merge of one with other

this land now a ridge
    of palimpsest
estuarine text
    a redraft in the wash
of story

    it is imprint
of ocean-etch
continental   lock and
    shift,   mollusc

on summit,   postscript
    left by a long dragging   back
                an inch by inch revision

where valley and cwm
        are marginalia
shores a subordinate
        clause in each edit
                of coastline

a confluent narrative,   land
        under water under land
                re-structured like
language, staying
                        hidden, yet
                                speaking out loud.

Breathing lessons

I am learning how
to breathe. Underwater.
Life's harsh wish

makes my corpuscles
bloat, blood strobes,
the whole of an ocean

holds me. Down here,
the reef's a temple
or a church, filled

with aisles of kelp,
aslant with stained-
glass shafts of sun, pale

haloes of medusae.
Flocks of fish kiss
digits of coral,

fins steadying for
benediction. I kneel
to join the swaying

congregations, but
they blanch, shiver
into vanished blue.

The surface
does not satisfy,
I must deepen,

though my lungs
are in denial
of the rationing

of air, too long used
to living in the dry.
An apprentice

to these depths,
I cling to oxygen
like clinging to God,

my apparatus rattles
and ticks—I gulp,
a supplicant.

My breaths blister upward,
empty into light.
Is this why I've come

so deep? To learn
instead of oxygen,
belief? I unbuckle

my weights, shrug from
the grip of the skins.
Letting go of my mask

is hard, but then—
all the air I need
rushes in

River(l)ine

When the river goes underground it isn't lying
                                    James Galvin

When the river goes underground it isn't lying
    when
            the river goes under, the ground sighs,
                goes
  asunder, the river wends lines and grows sly gerunds
    under
            the lining we shiver a riff, we are groundlings
            we sigh
   as the giver rows in reverse
 what
lies under the river?
   will we
           grow lives round a verse if the rivets shift?
                    or
            will we end?
            when
the reverie enlivens a given it isn't going to lie
    the roundelay
            undergoes a wounding, becomes a riven anaglyph
                that
                glows underground like
          vernix
      we
   are sly, we eviscerate the when of ending
under
 the river grows a glyph
    we
         shift our lives to lie around

Notes and acknowledgements

I am grateful to the editors of the journals and anthologies in which some of these poems (or versions of them) were originally published: *Australian Love Poems* (Inkerman & Blunt), *Cordite Poetry Review*, *Cuttlefish, Desde Hong Kong: Poets in conversation with Octavio Paz* (Chameleon Press), *Rabbit Poetry Journal, Imprint, Poetry D'Amour, Westerly Journal, The Golden Shovel Anthology* (University of Arksansas Press), and *Afterness: Literature from the New Transnational Asia* (After-Party Press, Hong Kong).

Some of the poems in this collection have also been successful in competitions and I am grateful for the encouragement such opportunities provide.

My profound thanks go to David Musgrave, Ann Vickery and Ross Gillett of Puncher and Wattmann for their help in publishing this collection, and to everyone (especially Cassandra Atherton) who has offered support, inspiration and encouragement along the way. Many of these poems were written during a three-year period of living in Hong Kong, an experience that taught me so much in so many ways. My gratitude and affection go in particular to the faculty and students of the sadly now defunct MFA program in Creative Writing at City University of Hong Kong, especially Xu Xi, Tina Chang, Marilyn Chin, Sharmistha Mohanty, Luis H. Francia, Ravi Shankar, Suzanne Paola, Miho Kinnas, Sarah Vallance, Hayley Katzen, Gershom Tse, and Ciriaco Offedu.

I

I know you'd rather I stayed hidden

Hybrid: The quotation comes from Alice Oswald's poem 'Narcissus' in *Weeds and Wildflowers*, (Faber and Faber 2009)

Bonnard beauty reveals all: inspired by the canvases of Pierre Bonnard (1867–1947)

Metabolising Heathcliff: This poem is after Liz Lochhead's 'Dreaming Frankenstein' published in *Dreaming Frankenstein & Collected Poems 1967–1984* (Polygon Books 1984)

Dolores: Vladimir Nabokov, author of *Lolita*, was a keen lepidopterist, hence the poem's reference to the butterfly effect. Dolores (the Spanish word for pain) is Lolita's real name

Inside the ghost mind: Emily Dickinson's quotation comes from poem #670 in *Complete Poems* (Faber and Faber 1970)

Jessie from the Golden Shovel: the words at the end of each line echo Gwendolyn Brooks' poem 'We Real Cool: The Pool Players: Seven at the Golden Shovel' available at the Poetry Foundation website

Mrs Batman M.D, Msc, Psych.D: inspired by Carol Ann Duffy's collection *The World's Wife*, (Picador 1999)

II

Nothing to declare

you voyage my body: inspired by the poem 'Sun stone' by Octavio Paz (1914–1998), *Collected Poems of Octavio Paz* (New Directions 1987)

cinq à sept: literally 'five to seven,' this refers to the period when lovers meet between leaving the office and returning to the family home.

Sappho's italicised quotations come from her fragments 'Prayer to Afroditi,' 'Comparisons,' 'Behind a Laurel Tree'

III

Pauses in transit

Pauses in transit: inspired by 'Between going and staying' by Octavio Paz, *Collected Poems of Octavio Paz* (New Directions 1987)

Different skin: Lo Fu Tau is a hill (also known as Tiger's Head) on Lantau Island, Hong Kong. *xíngshū* is running or cursive script

Sinister: this poem was inspired by reading Tracy Ryan's 'Poem Written With The Left Hand' in *The Argument*, (Fremantle Press 2011)

IV

Recovered memory

The Before & in the After: The quotation comes from Lavinia Greenlaw's poem 'Snow Line' in *A World Where News Travelled Slowly*, (Faber and Faber 1997)

Sleeper: the quotation is by Roger Deakin, from *Wildwood: A Journey Through Trees* (Hamish Hamilton 2008)

V

Breathing lessons

Source: this poem references the season sequence of the northern hemisphere.

Nostos: this poem references 'Ithaka' by Greek poet C.P. Cavafy (1863–1933)

Displacement: Rainer Maria Rilke's quotation comes from *Letters to a Young Poet* (Penguin Classics 2012)

Only butterflies: Mahmoud Darwish (1941–2008) was a Palestinian poet and author. 'To a Young Poet' begins: *Don't believe our outlines, forget them/ and begin from your own words. / As if you are the first to write poetry/ or the last poet.* (translated by Fady Joudah and available at the Poetry Foundation website)

River(l)ine: This quotation comes from his James Galvin's poem 'Leap Year' which appears in *American Hybrid: a Norton Anthology of New Poetry*, (Norton 2009).

www.ingramcontent.com/pod-product-compliance
Lightning Source LLC
Chambersburg PA
CBHW030852090426
42737CB00009B/1205